THE GEMINI EFFECT: GOOGLE'S AI MASTERPIECE

Discovering the Secrets of the Most Advanced AI Model.

Antonio Martín

CONTENTS

Disclaimer

This eBook has been created with the assistance of artificial intelligence (AI). The content within this eBook is based on publicly available information, hypothetical scenarios, and predictive analysis regarding Google's Gemini AI software. It is important for readers to note that:

1. Accuracy and Currentness: While every effort has been made to ensure the accuracy and currentness of the information, AI-generated content may contain inaccuracies, outdated information, or speculative predictions that may not align with future developments.

2. Hypothetical Scenarios: Much of the content regarding the applications and implications of Google Gemini is based on hypothetical scenarios. As Gemini is not yet widely released or used, these scenarios are predictive in nature and should not be considered definitive or factual representations of Gemini's capabilities.

3. No Endorsement by Google: This eBook and its content are not endorsed by or affiliated with Google. The views and interpretations presented herein are those generated by AI and do not reflect the official policy or position of Google or its subsidiaries.

4. Purpose of the eBook: This eBook is intended for informational and educational purposes only. It is aimed at technology enthusiasts and individuals interested in AI advancements but should not be used as a sole source for decision-making related to technology investments, development, or adoption.

5. Changes and Updates: The field of AI is rapidly evolving. As such, the content pertaining to Gemini and related technologies may change. Readers are encouraged to consult additional sources and stay updated with official releases from Google for the latest information.

6. No Liability: The creators of this eBook and the AI used to generate its content bear no responsibility for any errors, inaccuracies, or outdated information and will not be liable for any decisions or actions taken based on the information provided.

By continuing to read this eBook, you acknowledge and accept the limitations and disclaimers noted above.

INTRODUCTION

Stay always up-to-date with the latest information! By purchasing this book, you're getting much more than just a one-time read: I'm offering you free updates to ensure you always have access to the most recent and relevant content. How does it work? It's simple:

1. Scan the **QR Code** below.
2. Send Us You**r Order Number**.
3. Get **Updates** Straight to Your **Email:** Once registered, you'll automatically receive the latest updates and improvements to the book.

Overview Of The Ai Landscape And The Significance Of Google's Entry With Gemini

The landscape of artificial intelligence (AI) has been rapidly evolving, marked by significant advancements and innovations.

This field, once dominated by theoretical research, has transitioned into practical applications impacting various sectors, including technology, healthcare, finance, and more. Within this dynamic environment, Google's introduction of its AI model, Gemini, represents a pivotal moment. Gemini's arrival signals a new chapter in AI development, showcasing Google's commitment to advancing the frontiers of technology.

Gemini, as a multimodal AI model, distinguishes itself by its ability to process and understand a diverse range of information types, including text, images, video, audio, and code. This versatility positions Gemini at the forefront of AI development, promising to surpass existing models like GPT-4 in various aspects. Google's foray into this advanced AI realm with Gemini is not just a technological triumph but also a strategic move to maintain its leadership in the competitive AI market.

Brief History Of Ai Development At Google, Leading Up To Gemini

Google's journey in AI has been marked by continuous innovation and a deep commitment to pushing the boundaries of what's possible. The company's AI development trajectory can be traced back to its foundational algorithms that revolutionized internet search. Over the years, Google has consistently been at the forefront of AI research, developing technologies like machine learning, natural language processing, and neural networks.

The formation of Google DeepMind was a significant milestone, further solidifying Google's position as a leader in AI research. DeepMind's breakthroughs in reinforcement learning and neural network design have been instrumental in shaping the current AI landscape. The development of Gemini is a culmination of these efforts, leveraging Google's rich history in AI to create a model that sets new standards in multimodal AI capabilities.

Objectives Of The Ebook And Its Relevance To Tech Enthusiasts

This eBook aims to provide a comprehensive guide to Google's Gemini AI software, from its inception to its latest developments and applications. It is designed to cater to technology enthusiasts, AI researchers, software developers, and anyone interested in the rapidly evolving field of artificial intelligence.

Readers can expect in-depth analyses of Gemini's capabilities, insights into its potential applications, and a detailed understanding of how it compares to other AI models. The eBook also explores the broader implications of Gemini's advancements for the future of AI and technology as a whole. By delving into the technical, ethical, and practical aspects of Gemini, this eBook will serve as an essential resource for anyone keen to stay abreast of the latest trends and developments in AI technology.

CHAPTER 1: THE BIRTH OF GEMINI

1.1 Exploration of the Initial Concept and Development of Gemini

The genesis of Google Gemini was not a standalone endeavor but the culmination of decades of exploration and innovation in artificial intelligence at Google. This journey in AI began with the foundational mission to organize the world's information, leading to groundbreaking developments in algorithmic intricacies and machine learning through projects like Google Brain and DeepMind.

Gemini, however, marks a distinct chapter in Google's AI narrative. It represents an amalgamation of Google's accumulated knowledge, experience, and foresight in AI. Born from the aspiration to transcend the traditional limitations of AI, Gemini was envisioned as a multifaceted AI solution. Its core idea was to integrate multiple modalities of human interaction – text, image, audio, and video – to understand and interact with the world in an unprecedented computing manner.

1.2 Insights into Google DeepMind's Vision for Gemini

At the heart of Gemini lies a vision that transcends technological prowess. Google, with Gemini, aimed to create an AI that is not just computationally powerful but also intuitively understands the world, mirroring the multifaceted nature of human intelligence. The vision for Gemini was to craft an AI that empowers and enriches human life, bridging the gap between human and machine interaction.

The objectives behind Gemini were manifold. They included achieving universal understanding by breaking down silos between different AI models, emphasizing ethical AI to ensure fairness, privacy, and transparency, and creating real-world impact across various sectors. Google envisioned Gemini as a collaborative platform, integrating inputs from academia, industry experts, and public feedback, ensuring it evolves as a tool for societal betterment.

1.3 Description of the Multimodal Capabilities of Gemini

Gemini stands out for its ability to provide a unified and comprehensive understanding of diverse data types. It breaks the traditional mold of AI models that specialize in either text, audio, or visual inputs. Instead, Gemini is designed to seamlessly integrate and understand these various forms of data, offering a more holistic and nuanced understanding of information.

In practical terms, Gemini's multimodal capabilities mean it can process and interpret data from different sources simultaneously. This ability makes it uniquely positioned to handle complex tasks that require a combination of textual understanding, visual interpretation, audio processing, and more. Such a comprehensive approach allows Gemini to function in diverse applications, ranging from healthcare diagnostics to enhancing educational tools, improving environmental monitoring, and transforming entertainment experiences.

In the next chapters, we will explore in detail each of these facets of Gemini, unraveling how it redefines our understanding of artificial intelligence and its potential to shape the future.

CHAPTER 2: UNDERSTANDING GEMINI'S MULTIMODAL NATURE

2.1 Detailed Explanation of What Multimodal AI Means

In the realm of artificial intelligence, "multimodal" refers to the ability of an AI system to interpret and integrate multiple types of data input simultaneously. This approach contrasts with unimodal systems, which specialize in processing just one type of data, such as text or images. Multimodal AI, like Google's Gemini, can understand a combination of text, images, video, audio, and code. This integration reflects a more holistic approach to AI, mirroring the complex way humans perceive and interact with the world.

The essence of multimodal AI lies in its ability to not only process these diverse data types but to synthesize them into a coherent understanding. This synthesis allows for more nuanced responses and solutions, mirroring human cognitive processes more closely than unimodal systems.

2.2 How Gemini Integrates Text, Code, Audio, Image, and Video Processing

Gemini's architecture is designed to seamlessly integrate and process different data types. This integration is achieved through sophisticated machine learning algorithms and neural network models that can handle the intricacies of each data type while finding the interconnections between them.

- Text and Code: Gemini's text and code processing capabilities are grounded in its understanding of natural language and programming languages. It can interpret and generate human and machine languages, facilitating tasks like code generation, debugging, and language translation.

- Audio: Gemini's audio processing extends beyond mere speech recognition. It encompasses understanding the context, sentiment, and nuances in spoken language, enabling it to interact in a conversational manner or analyze audio data for insights.

- Image and Video: For image and video, Gemini employs advanced computer vision techniques to not only recognize objects and scenes but also to understand the context and the story they convey. This capability is pivotal in applications like medical imaging, environmental monitoring, and content creation.

2.3 Comparisons with Previous AI Models to Highlight Advancements

When compared to previous AI models, Gemini stands out for its advanced integration of multiple data types. While models like OpenAI's GPT-4 have made significant strides in natural language processing and generation, Gemini's multimodal approach allows it to go a step further.

- Against Text-centric Models: Unlike models primarily focused on text, Gemini's ability to understand and generate multimedia content offers a more comprehensive AI solution. This capability is particularly crucial in scenarios where context is derived from a combination of text, visuals, and audio.

- In Comparison to Specialized Models: Compared to specialized models that excel in either image recognition or speech processing, Gemini's integrated approach allows for more versatile and context-aware applications. For instance, in a healthcare setting, Gemini can analyze medical reports (text), patient interviews (audio), and imaging scans (visuals) in tandem to provide more accurate diagnoses.

Gemini's development marks a significant leap in AI capabilities, moving towards a more integrated and contextually aware system. As we explore further, we will delve into the specific applications and real-world impacts of these advancements.

CHAPTER 3: GEMINI'S PERFORMANCE BENCHMARKS

3.1 Examination of Gemini's Performance Across Various Benchmarks

Google Gemini has undergone rigorous testing across a spectrum of benchmarks to validate its capabilities and performance. These benchmarks are crucial for assessing the model's proficiency in handling diverse tasks and its ability to outperform existing AI models in various domains.

One key area of evaluation for Gemini has been its ability to understand and process multimodal data. The performance of Gemini is not just measured by its accuracy in understanding text or images individually but also by how effectively it integrates and interprets these modalities in unison. This comprehensive testing approach ensures that Gemini's performance is evaluated in scenarios that closely mimic real-world applications.

3.2 Discussion on Gemini Ultra's Achievements in MMLU and Other Tests

Gemini Ultra, the most advanced iteration of the Gemini series, has shown remarkable results, particularly in the Massive Multitask Language Understanding (MMLU) benchmark. MMLU is a comprehensive test that evaluates an AI model's understanding across a wide range of subjects, including math, physics, history, law, and ethics. Gemini Ultra's performance in this benchmark has been noteworthy, consistently outperforming human experts and setting a new standard in AI language understanding.

In addition to MMLU, Gemini Ultra has been tested on other critical benchmarks that assess its capabilities in natural image and video understanding, mathematical reasoning, and complex problem-solving. These tests are designed to push the boundaries of what AI models can achieve, and Gemini Ultra's success in these areas underscores its advanced capabilities.

3.3 Comparison of Gemini's Capabilities with GPT-4 and Other AI Models

When compared with other leading AI models like OpenAI's GPT-4, Gemini demonstrates several advancements. While GPT-4 is renowned for its language processing capabilities, Gemini extends beyond this by offering a more integrated approach to understanding and interacting with multiple data types.

- Text and Language Processing: Both Gemini and GPT-4 excel in language understanding and generation, but Gemini's ability to contextualize this within multimodal data sets it apart.

- Image and Video Processing: Unlike GPT-4, which primarily focuses on text, Gemini's proficiency in interpreting and analyzing images and videos adds a significant dimension to its capabilities.

- Integration and Contextual Understanding: Perhaps the most crucial difference lies in how Gemini integrates these different modalities to provide a more contextually rich and nuanced understanding, aligning more closely with human cognitive processes.

To summarize, Gemini's performance benchmarks highlight its position as a groundbreaking AI model, particularly in its ability to handle multimodal data and provide comprehensive, context-aware solutions.

CHAPTER 4: APPLICATIONS OF GEMINI IN REAL-WORLD SCENARIOS

4.1 Possible Applications of Gemini in Various Fields

As Gemini is a groundbreaking AI model, its potential applications span across multiple sectors. While it has not yet been implemented in real-world scenarios, here are some envisioned applications:

1. Automotive Industry: Gemini could revolutionize autonomous driving technologies. By integrating and analyzing real-time data from various sensors, traffic patterns, and environmental conditions, Gemini can enhance decision-making algorithms, making self-driving cars safer and more efficient.

2. Financial Sector: In finance, Gemini's ability to process complex financial reports, market trends, and economic indicators in multiple formats could provide deeper insights for investment strategies and risk assessment.

3. Legal and Compliance: For legal professionals, Gemini could assist in analyzing legal documents, case laws, and audiovisual material from court proceedings, thereby streamlining legal research and case preparation.

4. *etail and Customer Service: In retail, Gemini could be utilized to create more personalized shopping experiences by understanding customer preferences through a combination of textual feedback, browsing habits, and visual cues.

5. Language Translation and Cultural Interpretation: Gemini's advanced language processing capabilities, combined with its understanding of cultural nuances in visual and audio content,

could lead to more accurate and context-aware translation services.

6. Public Safety and Emergency Response: Gemini can play a vital role in disaster management and public safety by analyzing a wide range of data, including emergency calls, social media feeds, and satellite imagery, to assist in quicker and more effective response strategies.

7. Health and Wellness: In the health sector, Gemini's multimodal capabilities could enable the development of personalized health and wellness apps that consider a user's textual input, physiological data, and even emotional cues from voice and facial expressions.

8. Entertainment and Media: For the entertainment industry, Gemini could aid in content creation by analyzing current trends across text, audio, and visual media, helping creators to produce content that resonates with diverse audiences.

These possible applications of Gemini illustrate its potential to transform industries by providing more integrated, intelligent, and user-centric solutions.

4.2 Discussion on How Gemini Can Be Integrated into Existing Google Products and Services

Gemini's integration into Google's ecosystem is anticipated to revolutionize how users interact with Google's products and services. Potential integrations include:

1. Google Search: Enhancing search capabilities by providing more nuanced and contextually relevant results, including multimedia content.

2. Google Assistant: Upgrading the assistant with more natural and responsive conversational abilities, understanding queries in a more human-like manner.

3. YouTube: Improving content recommendation algorithms by understanding video content and user preferences more deeply.

4.3 Potential Future Applications and Their Implications

Looking ahead, the potential applications of Gemini are vast and varied:

1. Smart Cities: Gemini could be instrumental in the development of smart city solutions, analyzing a multitude of data sources for urban planning, traffic management, and public safety.

2. Creative Industries: In creative fields, Gemini could assist in generating music, art, and literature by understanding and integrating different artistic elements and styles.

3. Robotics and Automation: Integrating Gemini into robotics could lead to more intuitive and adaptable robots capable of performing complex tasks in dynamic environments.

The implications of these applications are profound, offering opportunities for innovation and improvement in quality of life, while also presenting challenges in terms of privacy, security, and ethical use of AI.

CHAPTER 5: GEMINI'S IMPACT ON CODING AND SOFTWARE DEVELOPMENT

5.1 Overview of Gemini's Coding Capabilities and Language Support

Gemini, although not yet released for widespread use, is anticipated to significantly influence the coding and software development landscape. Its potential capabilities in understanding and generating code in various programming languages, including Python, Java, C++, and Go, suggest a new era in software development. Gemini is expected to understand complex code structures, algorithms, and even assist in debugging and optimizing code, making it a valuable tool for developers.

Moreover, Gemini's proficiency in language support extends beyond just programming languages. Its capacity to process natural language and integrate it with code generation implies a more intuitive interface for developers, potentially transforming how coding and software development are approached.

5.2 Introduction of AlphaCode and its Integration with Gemini

One of the most exciting prospects for Gemini in software development is its integration with systems like AlphaCode. AlphaCode, developed by DeepMind, represents a significant advancement in AI-driven code generation. The integration of Gemini with AlphaCode could lead to even more sophisticated coding solutions, where Gemini's multimodal capabilities enhance AlphaCode's programming proficiency.

This integration is expected to facilitate the creation of more advanced AI-driven coding tools, capable of not just generating code but also providing intelligent suggestions, optimizations, and even creative programming solutions based on a deep understanding of various data inputs.

5.3 The Potential Impact of Gemini on the Software Development Landscape

The introduction of Gemini into the software development world holds the promise of a paradigm shift. Its potential impacts include:

- Enhanced Productivity: By automating routine coding tasks and offering intelligent coding suggestions, Gemini could significantly boost developer productivity.

- Improved Code Quality: Gemini's ability to analyze and learn from vast codebases could lead to higher-quality code generation and fewer errors.

- Cross-language Development: With its language-agnostic approach, Gemini could facilitate development across multiple programming languages, making it easier to manage multi-language projects.

- Educational Tool: For novice programmers, Gemini could serve as an educational tool, offering guidance and learning resources based on its understanding of coding patterns and best practices.

- Innovative Solutions: Gemini could enable the development of novel software solutions by combining its understanding of different modalities, such as integrating visual data processing with code generation for more intuitive user interfaces.

As Gemini evolves, its exact impact on coding and software

development will become clearer, potentially heralding a new era of AI-assisted programming.

CHAPTER 6:
THE TECHNICAL
MARVEL BEHIND
GEMINI

6.1 Technical Discussion on the Architecture of Gemini, Including Its Use of TPUs and GPUs

Gemini's architecture represents a fusion of cutting-edge technology and innovative AI design. While specific details of Gemini's architecture are yet to be fully disclosed, it is anticipated to leverage Google's advancements in Tensor Processing Units (TPUs) and Graphics Processing Units (GPUs).

- Tensor Processing Units (TPUs): TPUs, designed by Google, are custom-built to accelerate machine learning workloads. They are particularly effective in handling the large-scale matrix operations common in neural network training and inference. For Gemini, TPUs would provide the computational power necessary to process multimodal data efficiently, allowing the model to learn and respond faster than traditional hardware.

- Graphics Processing Units (GPUs): Alongside TPUs, GPUs are expected to play a crucial role in Gemini's architecture. GPUs are adept at handling parallel processing tasks, making them suitable for the intensive computations required in training and running sophisticated AI models like Gemini. The combination of TPUs and GPUs would enable Gemini to achieve high levels of efficiency and speed.

6.2 Insights into the Training and Efficiency of Gemini Models

The training process of Gemini is hypothesized to be a monumental task, given its multimodal nature. It would involve:

- Large-scale Data Processing: Gemini would require extensive training on vast datasets encompassing text, images, videos, and audio to achieve its multimodal capabilities. This training would likely be iterative, with continuous refinements to improve accuracy and performance.

- Efficiency Considerations: Despite the massive computational requirements, efficiency is a critical aspect of Gemini's design. The use of TPUs and GPUs not only enhances processing speed but also optimizes energy consumption. This efficiency is vital for making Gemini scalable and practical for widespread use.

- Continuous Learning and Updating: To remain effective and relevant, Gemini would need to continually update its learning base, adapting to new data and evolving use cases. This aspect of Gemini's design underscores the model's dynamic and ever-improving nature.

The technical architecture of Gemini, with its sophisticated use of TPUs and GPUs, underscores Google's commitment to pushing the boundaries of AI capabilities. The model's training and efficiency highlight the intricate balance between power and practicality, setting a new standard in the AI landscape.

CHAPTER 7: SAFETY, SECURITY, AND ETHICAL CONSIDERATIONS

7.1 Analysis of Google's Approach to Ensuring the Safety and Security of Gemini

As Gemini represents a significant leap in AI technology, Google's approach to ensuring its safety and security is paramount. Predictively, Google would employ robust mechanisms to safeguard Gemini from potential misuse and ensure its alignment with ethical standards. This could include:

- Advanced Security Protocols: Implementing state-of-the-art security measures to protect Gemini from unauthorized access and cyber threats.

- Data Privacy and Integrity: Upholding strict data privacy policies to ensure the confidentiality and integrity of the data processed by Gemini.

- Continuous Monitoring and Auditing: Regularly monitoring Gemini's performance and decision-making processes for any signs of bias, error, or unintended consequences.

7.2 *Discussion on Ethical Considerations in the Deployment of Gemini*

The deployment of Gemini brings with it a host of ethical considerations, especially given its advanced capabilities. It is anticipated that Google would address these concerns through:

- Bias Mitigation: Ensuring that Gemini's training data is diverse and representative to avoid biases in its outputs.

- Transparency and Explainability: Making Gemini's decision-making processes transparent and understandable to users, fostering trust in the AI system.

- Ethical AI Frameworks: Adhering to ethical AI frameworks that guide the development and deployment of Gemini, ensuring it benefits society while minimizing harm.

7.3 Overview of Google's AI Principles in the Context of Gemini

Google's AI Principles, which emphasize social benefits, safety, privacy, and fairness, would play a crucial role in the development and deployment of Gemini. These principles would guide the design and application of Gemini, ensuring it aligns with Google's commitment to responsible AI development. Key aspects would likely include:

- Beneficial: Leveraging Gemini's capabilities to address societal challenges and improve people's lives.

- Avoiding Unfair Bias: Striving to prevent unfair bias in Gemini, ensuring it's inclusive and equitable in its functionality.

- Accountability and Governance: Establishing clear accountability and governance structures to oversee Gemini's deployment and use.

In summary, the safety, security, and ethical considerations surrounding Gemini are integral to its development and deployment. Google's commitment to these principles is expected to shape Gemini into a responsible and beneficial AI technology.

CHAPTER 8: GEMINI IN EVERYDAY LIFE

8.1 Exploration of How Gemini Can Be Used in Daily Activities and Tasks

Gemini, with its advanced AI capabilities, has the potential to significantly impact daily life. Although not yet in widespread use, the following are hypothetical ways Gemini could integrate into everyday activities:

1. Personalized Information Retrieval: Gemini could enhance personal digital assistants, providing more accurate and context-aware responses to queries, making information retrieval more efficient and personalized.

2. Smart Home Integration: In smart home environments, Gemini could manage devices and systems more intuitively, understanding complex voice commands and even non-verbal cues like gestures or facial expressions.

3. Enhanced Educational Tools: For students and educators, Gemini could offer a more interactive and personalized learning experience, adapting to individual learning styles and providing multimodal educational content.

4. Health and Fitness: Gemini's potential in personalized health and fitness apps is significant. It could provide tailored health advice and fitness routines by analyzing a combination of health metrics, dietary preferences, and lifestyle data.

8.2 Discussion on Gemini's Integration into Consumer Products like Google Pixel and Bard

Gemini's integration into consumer products could revolutionize user experiences:

1. Google Pixel Integration: Gemini could enhance the functionality of Google Pixel smartphones, offering advanced features like real-time language translation, sophisticated image and video analysis, and intuitive voice commands.

2. Bard Integration: In Google's Bard, Gemini's capabilities could lead to a more conversational and insightful AI chatbot, capable of understanding and responding to complex queries with a depth of understanding that surpasses current standards.

8.3 Anticipated Future Developments and Updates to Gemini

The future of Gemini promises continual advancements and updates, such as:

- Adaptive Learning: Gemini's ability to learn and adapt to user preferences and behaviors could continually evolve, offering more personalized and relevant interactions.

- Cross-Platform Integration: Gemini could extend its reach across multiple platforms and devices, providing a seamless and integrated AI experience.

- Advanced Multimodal Interactions: Future updates could see Gemini handling more complex multimodal interactions, such as interpreting emotional cues in voice and video, leading to more empathetic and human-like AI interactions.

- Collaborative Tools: Gemini could become a collaborative tool in professional settings, assisting in tasks ranging from design and creativity to data analysis and decision-making.

In summary, the potential integration of Gemini into daily life and consumer products could lead to significant enhancements in how we interact with technology, making it more intuitive, efficient, and personalized.

CHAPTER 9: THE FUTURE OF AI WITH GEMINI

9.1 Predictions and Expectations for the Future Development of Gemini

As Gemini represents a groundbreaking advancement in AI, its future development is expected to be marked by continuous innovation. Predictive insights into Gemini's evolution suggest:

1. Enhanced Multimodal Integration: Future versions of Gemini may achieve even more seamless integration of diverse data types, further blurring the lines between text, audio, visual, and code-based AI interactions.

2. Greater Contextual Understanding: Future iterations could exhibit enhanced contextual awareness, interpreting not just the content but also the intent and nuances of user interactions.

3. Adaptive Learning Algorithms: Gemini may evolve to include more sophisticated self-learning algorithms, allowing it to adapt more dynamically to user preferences and changes in data patterns.

9.2 Potential Advancements in AI and Their Societal Impact

The advancements brought about by Gemini have the potential to revolutionize various aspects of society:

- Healthcare: With more accurate and intuitive AI, Gemini could assist in diagnostics, personalized treatment plans, and monitoring patient health, leading to improved healthcare outcomes.

- Education: Gemini could offer personalized learning experiences, adapting to individual learning styles and needs, thus revolutionizing the educational landscape.

- Environmental Conservation: AI models like Gemini could analyze vast environmental data sets, aiding in climate change research and conservation efforts.

9.3 Google's Roadmap and Vision for the Future of AI

Google's roadmap for AI, with Gemini at its core, likely includes:

1. Continued Innovation: Google is expected to continue its trajectory of groundbreaking research and development in AI, with Gemini being a central focus.

2. Ethical AI Development: A commitment to ethical AI development, ensuring that advancements like Gemini are aligned with societal values and norms.

3. Collaborative Growth: Google may seek to collaborate with various sectors and communities to ensure that the benefits of AI, particularly Gemini, are widely accessible and ethically implemented.

In summary, the future of AI with Gemini is poised to be a journey of innovative breakthroughs, societal impacts, and ethical considerations. Google's role in shaping this future will be crucial, with Gemini potentially setting new benchmarks in the AI domain.

CHAPTER 10: GETTING STARTED WITH GEMINI

10.1 Guide for Developers and Enterprises on Accessing and Using Gemini

As Google Gemini heralds a new era in AI, it presents an exciting opportunity for developers and enterprises. Although Gemini is not yet widely available, it is anticipated that access will be facilitated through various Google platforms. Developers and enterprises looking to utilize Gemini should prepare by:

1. Staying Informed: Keep abreast of official Google announcements regarding Gemini's availability. Subscribing to Google's AI and developer newsletters is a good way to stay updated.

2. Exploring Google AI Studio: Google AI Studio is likely to be a key platform for accessing Gemini. Familiarizing oneself with this environment will be beneficial.

3. Understanding Google Cloud Vertex AI: For more extensive applications, Google Cloud Vertex AI may offer advanced tools and infrastructure for integrating Gemini into larger projects.

10.2 Resources and Tools Available for Working with Gemini

While specific tools and resources for Gemini will be detailed upon its release, developers and enterprises can anticipate:

- API Access: Access to Gemini's functionalities via APIs will likely be a primary method for integration.

- Documentation and Guides: Comprehensive documentation, including implementation guides, best practices, and case studies, will likely be available to assist in leveraging Gemini's capabilities.

- Developer Forums and Support: Google may provide forums and support channels for developers to collaborate, share insights, and get assistance with Gemini-related queries.

10.3 Tips and Best Practices for Integrating Gemini into Various Applications

Integrating Gemini into applications, while hypothesized to be straightforward, will require adherence to best practices:

1. Data Privacy and Security: Ensure compliance with data privacy laws and Google's guidelines. Secure handling of data within Gemini applications will be paramount.

2. Testing and Validation: Rigorously test the integration of Gemini in various scenarios to ensure it performs as expected and enhances the application's capabilities.

3. Scalability and Efficiency: Consider the scalability of your applications with Gemini, especially in handling large datasets or complex multimodal interactions.

4. User Experience: Design applications keeping in mind the enhanced capabilities of Gemini, aiming for intuitive and seamless user interactions.

5. Ethical Use: Align the application's use of Gemini with ethical AI principles, ensuring that it is used to benefit users without causing harm or bias.

By following these guidelines, developers and enterprises can prepare to effectively harness the power of Gemini, paving the way for innovative applications and solutions.

CONCLUSION

This eBook has embarked on a comprehensive journey through the realms of Google Gemini, a transformative AI model poised to redefine the AI landscape. We've explored:

1. The Genesis of Gemini: Delving into its multimodal nature, we've understood how Gemini's innovative approach sets it apart from predecessors like GPT-4.

2. Technical Prowess: The discussion on Gemini's architecture revealed its use of advanced TPUs and GPUs, highlighting its efficiency and potential for large-scale applications.

3. Safety and Ethics: We examined Google's commitment to responsible AI development, ensuring that Gemini adheres to ethical standards and safety measures.

4. Real-World Applications: While Gemini is not yet in widespread use, we've speculated on its potential impact across various sectors, from healthcare to software development.

5. Getting Started with Gemini: For developers and enterprises, we've provided a guide to accessing and using Gemini, underscoring the importance of ethical usage and data privacy.

Reflection On The Potential Of Gemini And Its Role In Advancing Ai

Gemini, with its groundbreaking capabilities, is not just another AI model; it represents a significant leap forward in the field of artificial intelligence. Its ability to process and integrate diverse data types positions it as a critical tool for future innovations. Gemini's potential to transform industries, enhance personal experiences, and contribute to societal advancement is immense.

Encouragement For Readers To Explore And Engage With Gemini

As we stand on the cusp of this new AI era, it's an exciting time for technology enthusiasts, developers, and enterprises alike. The prospective rollout of Gemini offers a unique opportunity to be part of a transformative journey. We encourage readers to stay informed about Gemini's developments, explore its capabilities upon release, and consider how this powerful AI model can be leveraged in your own domains of interest.

This eBook aims not only to inform but also to inspire. As Gemini evolves, it invites us to rethink our approach to AI, embrace new possibilities, and envision a future where technology and human intelligence converge in unprecedented ways.